ROAD WORK AHEAD
poems

◆

RAYMOND LUCZAK

◆

SiblingRivalryPress

Road Work Ahead: Poems.
Copyright © 2011 by Raymond Luczak.

Front cover photograph, "The Road to Court Hill," by Angus Clyne.
Used by permission (www.angusclyne.co.uk).

Back cover photograph by Raymond Luczak. Used by permission.

Cover design by Mona Z. Kraculdy.

Sibling Rivalry Press, LLC
13913 Magnolia Glen Drive
Alexander, AR 72002

www.siblingrivalrypress.com

Library of Congress Control Number: 2010939622

ISBN: 978-0-578-07158-9

First Sibling Rivalry Press Edition, March 2011

ACKNOWLEDGMENTS

The author wishes to thank the editors of these publications, where earlier
versions of these poems appeared:

Art & Understanding: "In Repose."
Assaracus: "Inevitability, 2005."
Brooklyn Review: "Trois Canards."
Chiron Review: "In That Dark of Night."
Creamdrops: "The Language of Sleep" (originally titled "Bed Language")
    and "Luminescences."
Deaf Arts UK: "Ascending the Matterhorn," "Kellys Island," and "Road
    Work Ahead" (originally titled "The Road Home").
Gallaudet Today: "Moss in Muir Woods" and "On a Greenpoint Pier."
The Gay & Lesbian Review Worldwide: "Pirates."
Kiss-Fist: "In Edinburgh Castle."
Lodestar Quarterly: "Farewell to A.R., 1990" (originally titled "Farewell
    Sestina to A.R.").
New York Native: "Dupont Circle, 3 A.M."
Poetic Voices Without Borders (Robert L. Giron, ed., Gival Press): "I Am a
    Shoe."
RFD: "Rehoboth Beach, 1985."
SIGNews: "Keepsake" (originally titled "First Love's Keepsake").
The Tactile Mind Quarterly: "The Ache of Alchemy," "After Suddenly Seeing
    A.R. Again," "Exchanging Beds," "On the 6 to Parkchester," "Shroud,"
    and "Sweet Highway."

An abundance of thanks goes to Bryan Borland and John Lee Clark for
    their keen insights on the poems within.

CONTENTS

"Twenty years from now you will be more disappointed by the things that you didn't do than by the ones you did do. So throw off the bowlines. Sail away from the safe harbor. Catch the trade winds in your sails. Explore. Dream. Discover."

— Mark Twain

for T.S.,
who's traveled more in my heart than anyone

ARC DE TRIOMPHE, 2005

Once I arrived in Paris, I declared war against Time.
That November I marched nonstop days and nights
up and down snow-slicked avenues and streets.

Spies adored my aging face. It'd given away
one secret after another. I had been shafted.
Journalists never covered my side of the story.

On the Avenue des Champs-Élysées, I was on parade,
but Time, drunk and happy, had been too busy
snapping photographs. My beret wasn't enough.

The Arc de Triomphe rose tall like a general.
Its sculptured reliefs stood proudly like epaulets.
Its tourist army was electrified like moths.

Underneath its arch of carved stone, a flame burned
eternal for the bones of an unknown soldier. How
odd that a faceless man could have so many friends!

Napoleon Bonaparte, the wily rascal that he was,
had calculated that stone reshaped to honor the dead was
his best shot against Time. So far he's winning.

FAREWELL TO A.R., 1990

Yes, it's now time for me to go.
The frame glass of your image has cracked but I have packed
    the memories deep inside my heart.
When I met you, you were thirty-two. I was only twenty-three.
    I had left a dull city, my first lover,
and a cheap apartment for New York where in no time
    I felt so much older than my time.
When I saw you, my entire body wanted to leap and go
    wherever you'd go. But did I want a lover?
I didn't know, but how your curious eyes could easily unpack
    the bundles of my soul . . . Never in my twenty-three
years had I felt so scared by anyone walking close by my heart.

Only now I realize I've never seen your heart.
Is it also a suitcase waiting to open at the right time?
    Was it as heavy as mine? At twenty-three
were you ever anxious as I was for a lover, to go
    anywhere to help him unpack
the suitcase of his heart? I thought you wanted a lover
    as much as I did. My perfect lover
had to be you, with your ocean-gray eyes, your mumbling heart,
    and your thick hands ready to unpack
and open the shutters halfway for some sunlight. In time,
    perhaps, you'd never want me to go.
But so much has happened since I went beyond twenty-three.

I'd never wish again to be twenty-three.
It was such a hard age, wanting you as the imperfect lover
    who'd want to go where I wanted to go,
and wanting to write my first book with you as its heart.
    I envied you having gone to Europe two times
when I'd never applied for a passport. I wanted to pack
    my suitcases, and take you with me to unpack
the wonder of my senses overseas. At twenty-three
    I'd thought so much about that one time
we'd leaned towards the East River while fathers and lovers
    took pictures of the U.N. to their heart's
content. Once upon a time I regretted you had to go.

    Now someone else wants to unpack me as his lover;
no longer twenty-three, I've become cautious with my heart.
    You remain a closed suitcase. It's time I go.

ARRIVING IN NEW YORK

I stand and fidget in my chair as officials
peer at my passport. The office
is dry with stacks and stacks of reports
of love affairs misled astray. They compare
my slapdash scrapbook against my face:
how could it be that I've explored
the countries of men I have loved, where
beyond the blistering Sahara, across
the tundras of Mongolia, beyond
the Alleghenies, and somewhere in Kenya
I have learned the roads the heart must take
before it could claim itself ready
to endure? They cannot believe I could have
such a light suitcase, even after searching it
for insoluble proof that I am capable
of survival. But I'm tired of traveling
on next to nothing: I want to go back home,
our little square of land where he and I can
cultivate fruits of kisses, vegetables of hugs,
and rosebushes of steady fragrances.
I open my returned suitcase to check
the jumbled clothes of men I wore once proudly.
Trouble was, I outgrew them too fast.
My Nikon wearied of men who'd thought
affairs were the best solution for boredom.
I lock my suitcase when a grumpy official waves me
over to his desk. He looks one more time

at my passport and shakes his head before he stamps
the ink of his approval for my homeland.
I heave my suitcase aboard and find you've been
saving an empty window seat for me.
Our travel horror stories can wait another time.
We braid fingers as we feel the takeoff's roar
together toward East 11th Street.

LUMINESCENCES

Trucks thundered by your blinded bedroom window:
your eyelids did not flicker from light's slices.
The moon was enraptured, as I was,
with your round face. You hinted secret smiles.

What dreams were you dreaming? I thought of the moon
where I'd drive from dusk to dawn past craters,
but somehow all your friends who'd died knew
you'd find them there on the blue-lined summits.

There, you stood proudly from your moon buggy to
wave everyone from the luminous darkness.
"It's beautiful here," you whispered.
Gravity made the earth clouds swirl sadly.

I slept beside you, your warm glow (like babies
not yet aware of their effect on parents)
illuminating my hushed silence.
I love your body, a wonderful moon.

METAPHYSICS

Who knows why clouds fluff up when they see you
sauntering all the way down on Broadway
to your apartment? Who knows why birds say
with many trills your name? (They've noticed too.)
Who knows why the cold air seems warmer now
when I find myself thinking of you? Oh,
who knows why on cold nights you seem to glow?
Who knows why sweat becomes sweet on your brow?

You are the wind rushing in from the north,
the melody from the evergreens,
the slowly ceaseless fireplace warmth's sheen.
The metaphysics of distance drop forth
into nothingness when I see you with
arms waiting to hug, no longer a myth.

NIGHT BEFORE THANKSGIVING

New York has fallen into a lazy-susan-eyed sleep.
As I saunter west from St. Mark's Place to my home,
I think of you arriving by car in Ohio.

Right now you must be laughing and carrying on
with your sisters, while you and mother cook in her home.
Am I somewhere in your mind out there in Ohio?

Out here by the lonely piers on Hudson River,
the winds lull me into a make-believe home.
Tonight I cast a net for dreams of you in Ohio.

I am blessed: there are so many leaping in the air.
Your eyes, hands, thighs trawl me rivers home.
I long to shimmer in your arms in Ohio.

When I finally fall asleep, I climb the tallest tree
over there. You are a breathtaking river called home,
reflecting the prism of autumn beyond Ohio.

AUBADE

Your eyes do not flicker when I travel
my autobahn of hesitation, afraid to gamble
again on speeding up your 10-mph sleep.
Your contented silence makes me want to weep.
Your lazy smile slows me; I am humbled.

But your body is a Mack of warmth. I wobble
when I map my anxious body next to your bundle
of hair, neck, back, ass, thighs I want to keep.
    Your eyes do not flicker.

Yet deep in my soul I want to rebel,
my fingers aching to drive your muscles
until your speedometer begins to weep
and exhaust beautifully in a sweaty heap.
Yes, I understand how much you need the sleep.
But honey dear, I'm so horny. I *am* compelled . . .
    Your eyes do not flicker.

TROIS CANARDS

Trios of ducks came quacking from nowhere
in the restaurant. We were, well, surprised,
but we pretended not to notice them.

They were mere children running past tables,
chasing and twitching their tails and chortling.
All their white wings flew into a spottle.

They leaped onto the table before us,
stretching up to a sudden opening
above. Arms big as night swooped down and took.

Where had they gone? We looked at our menus.
Gusts of wind flew in and carried us up.
Exploding clouds, we saw the Seine below.

A thousand quacks became a symphony,
twitches of tails as Paris lit alive.

ORBIT

How could the moon ever turn my face
when it comes to you, my heart's place?
Your eyes shimmer better than Venus
and inspire me to elliptical lusts.
My body reacts revolutions like Mercury
while you sweat like the sun next to me.
Instead I feel insulated from Neptune
as I melt in your arms, a sweet tune.
My heart's scrapbook is lost on Uranus:
suddenly it feels like a worn-out fuss.
You follow me, and I follow like Saturn,
and what else do I know? I've learned.
In our darkest moments, we see Mars
light aflame, healing our battle scars.
My fire has grown bigger than Jupiter
as I contemplate our bed's future.
No matter how wildly I may wander off,
you are my Earth, little planet of love.

FOR T.S., SLEEPING LATE IN NEW YORK

Your sandpaper stubble is now across the East River.
How I long to run my fingers through your Michelangelo curls,
weave them through your hands with a sculptor's eye,

and collect random recordings of your voice humming
phrases of music I've never heard. I miss your overtures—
a prelude to sweat atop sweat, a symphony of sensation: all

that begins with a never-enough kiss for that something more,
an ambivalence and the consummation of the certain wanting.
Must I check in my ticket and fly back to Ironwood? Oh no.

The giving of heart for a more potent blend, a mingling of legs,
tongues and arms: are these only words we imagine to be feeling?
Yes yes *yes* I seek that something more, as real as the soft knead

of your ass flexing under my fingers. Just to feel your chin
rubbing against my arm is temptation enough to change my flight.
Must the art of longing include the agony of newness?

SHOWER

Once there was an interminable winter.
The thrice-painted bathroom leaked icy drafts.
Even the mirror seemed to frost glazes.

The showerhead spewed near-icicles.
Naked with bloodless beads dripping, I stood
shivering and cursing the landlord.

The huge towel scratched my body dry.
My wet feet planted roots in the listless rug.
I caught myself unadorned in the mirror.

In that eternal moment you entered,
your hands kneading my shoulders. You
still gush warm water all over.

IN REPOSE

Let us all lie down with our ghosts long since
gone, drafts of cold air swirling around us.
We sleep in each other's arms, warm with trust,
while they have no place to atone their sins
committed so long ago they should know
when to let go. In the darkness we think
of all the incandescent ghosts who've linked
us together in the nightly soft glow,
and without speaking, we hold each other
in all the ways they need most to be held.
Their trivial obsessions are upheld
when they forget we're in this together
and go do they up the staircase of our
dreams where they disbelieve our warmth for hours.

KELLYS ISLAND

The day netted waves far
across the sturdy Lake Erie
as we four coasted our boat.

Behind us Lakeside's
whiteness was a vacated memory,
one more Labor Day past.

We skirted the docks and shore
past bicycles and golf carts
slowly weaving forth loose threads.

The tiny cluster of awnings
welcomed us inside for a table
of perch sandwiches and fries.

Our feet traveled only two blocks
in to discover nothing much
except a local legend on CD.

On the way back we stopped
for peach ice cream. My tongue
awoke from its drowsy daydream.

The coldness perfected its warmth
all over: I felt buoyed enough
for one more day, one more island.

THE LANGUAGE OF SLEEP

Ease of years, understanding: two taps,
a time to let go for a turn of body,
shifting limbs around for comfort.
The bottom of our sheets slides loose;
on our sides we knit our chests.
Nights of nothing are the sweetest.

Silence travels along our skins.
The sensation of our hot breaths
entering unmapped terrain through gaps
endlessly changing, nudge our bodies,
like a faint flashlight searching. Synapses
entire between us remain familiar.

NEVER, MY LOVE, COULD I

Never, my love, could I sleep so
easily when away from you nights
after days of dense tensions nearing
the breaking point of temper.

My body craves that sleeping pill
overdosing my coldness with warmth
emanating from the ground zero

of your arms and hairy chest encircling,
trapped in the river of gold nuggets
waited to be panned, to be heated
all over again each night we cling.

Never, my man, could I sleep alone
that easily nights away on the road.
In the tiring distance you're still on standby.

THERE WE ARE

There we are: you have your routines,
and I mine. We are well-oiled machines.

You think of the palate, the tongue,
as you read cookbooks, both old and young.

I nurture lines dirtying the screen.
I polish my craft until its sheen is clean.

Comfortable in our own ways, we sit
on either side of the wall. Nothing to it.

How time flies in the face of familiarity,
and how we learn to turn blind to whom we see.

QUIETUDE

Turn your eyes off the Weather Channel.
You are swimming in perfect coolness
with Elsa curled back against your hip.
Let the fog of stillness settle on your toes.

Outside the windows may lash with rain,
or decorate with a few ounces of snow.
The sudden heat of an Indian summer wave
may moisten your walking soul.

Keep sailing straight ahead on course.
You're the perfect recipe for any feast,
right here and anywhere you are.
Love, let the floodgates open.

TELEGRAM

The ocean sweeps below from my cliff
as winds race from the swirling skies
darkening its blues and grays.
I watch the lightning flare
as the thunder tiptoes quietly.
The curtain of clouds does not part.
I close my eyes and feel the cold
seal the warm lips of my eyes,
keeping my flickering dreams shut.
All around me are whispers from afar,
from inside the slender silk cable
swooping up and down
on the rickety wooden poles
across the land of waiting
where I've lived all my days.
My heart beeps in a Morse code,
a lonely blinking light across the ocean.

THE UNMOORING

Our bed is an ocean of tides that changes
the ceaseless fickle of distance between us.
You are an anchored ship of memory.
I am only a scrappy little tugboat.

I spent many seasons in awe of your heft.
I trailed behind, puffing in your shadow.
I simply chugged the cargo of my fears
and looked to you for safe harbor.

Days I slipped out for light and air.
I felt the full throttle of my own engine.
Out on the waters I passed others of my kind
who too felt anchored to their bigger ships.

With them, I learned to barter my heart.
The sea was a black market of affection.
I smuggled my contraband odes
wandering from harbor to island and back.

Somehow I've become a bearded captain,
steering madly with twinkling delight
past atlases of mistakes into the night
out there. My eyes are clear constellations.

ASCENDING THE MATTERHORN

Our breaths dance and dissolve into puffs
as we await with tickets to board the rail
closer to the nosetip of the Matterhorn.
High above us are the crisp crags of white,
its boulderous underskin exposed to all.
The mountain's a monster, curled like a dog
asleep under the sheathy blanket of snow.
Our cable car lurches with a slight hiccup
as we begin our winding ascent to the gods.
They have unleashed forces much larger
than we'd have ever imagined. The sharp
snow punctuates jarring flashes in my eyes.
Its brilliance penetrates my sunglasses.
My head hurts from the dull pain of waiting,
riding, and closing my eyelids for peace.
Inch by inch, we are climbing, breathing.
Thousands of meters high, my fear is so pure
that I'm no longer afraid to tumble down.
My sunglasses hide the avalanche of tears.

I AM A SHOE
for J.B.

I am a shoe in need of a right-sized foot. I ache
to have him slip inside me, wriggle his toes
comfortably as I walk with him everywhere.
No one would know how much I love him.

I know each crack of the cement ahead of me.
Each story of my past would surely break
my mother's back if she knew what I've done.
The feet in my life would trample her heart.

I am a shoe softened by fuzzy socks
that keep me warm and dry inside on
days that chill and nights that pour.
Each time a toe nudges me, I reawaken.

I am a shoe ready to itch from athlete's
foot. Secrets that shouldn't happen did.
I should be kicked every which way, but no,
the grass forgives me everything I am not.

EXCHANGING BEDS

Every night I soar to neverlands,
dreams never ending. The starry skies
shudder as I beg my eyelids to close.

I'm left with no place of arrival.
I've cast my old bed recklessly
into an ocean of rooms bobbing.

I have mapped boundaries of houses
I've slept in with mercury pillows.
The exchange rate of warmth is fickle.

Each bedroom is a country conquered:
souvenirs on shelves parade past me,
marching victories never my own.

Strange new beds underneath my body
is an idiom I can't master
quickly enough for my required dreams.

The air is an unearthly fragrance,
leaving my lungs to breathe the language
of ache. I need a new translation.

Nights I finger my passport. Still there.
Take me away from here. I belong
nowhere have I a bed to my name.

ON THE 6 TO PARKCHESTER

On the subway their faces were lit from below,
as if a warm fire had snaked from the pits
where the mole people had fanned
the first of its flames before the smoke leaked.
I stood silent, rocking and watching
the faces of the breathing dead flicker
occasionally from newspapers and books.
Words and images danced in their eyes,
now a hazy mirage in their far-off dreams,
a language in search of a dictionary.

I unleashed my hands, a burning tumbleweed,
through the car and saw them break free
from my own body. Yes, I did die:
my flying hands were caressing all their faces
like the first kiss of warmth on a winter's night.
As my body began to rot in the depths below,
and rolled over more each time the train lurched,
my bouncing palms collected tears as if in an ashtray
ready to laser the dead skin off their faces
until they turned translucent as newborns.

MISPLACED KISSES

Your first name was the shirt I stripped
    off you,
forgetting even
    the moment
how you appeared on my radar,
anonymous yet beguiling
    me close
enough to ask you
    for the time,
then undressing only with eyes.

We were simmering tea kettles
    on stove
the minute your tongue
    stirred me in
that mug of tea lingering,
eyes opening and closing
    in steam
of winter whistling
    finally
into the first blossoms of spring.

Your hands uprooted me, naked,
    hanging,
as my moist clumps of
    self-restraint
swung and fell to the morning earth

until I stood clean with the dewdrops
    of ache,
ready to plant my seed
    in gardens
always dreamed of but rarely seen.

One day we will pass on the street,
    daring
not to remember
    the scrapbook
we'd have stitched together
had we bothered to take pictures
    of us
not naked but wanting
    what we'd lost
when we each dreamed of someone else.

LOMBARD STREET, SAN FRANCISCO
for D.M.

A lifetime and half ago, I rode down
  the zigzags of Lombard Street, turning abruptly
    away from postcard houses tired of tourists
      and drunken out-of-towners driving past
        their perched houses all night long.
          With him I had felt a giddiness, a hope
        that maybe love had a chance,
      a fighting chance to erase
  my lingering doubts about him.
We zigzagged between cities and coasts
for years until I finally said: no.
  Time's left me wondering about him,
    who's never responded to any of my calls.
      There's nothing left between us
        except the water whispering.

Tonight I thought of you standing there
on top of Lombard Street. Your eyes
were lighthouses to mine, far stronger
than on Telegraph Hill beyond.
I wanted to drown in your giddiness
hinted at through the fog of crowds,
never wavering. If insecurity is a crime,
my heart would be sentenced forever
to the stony-faced Alcatraz. Your smile,
once prodding my deepest dreams awake
with never an anchor's peace,
have finally begun to ebb. Together
we could've sailed a straight line ahead.
But your foggy silence thunders to no one.
I shut my heart's foghorn off to forget.

SHROUD
after A.R.

Among streets swabbed with slickness
I feel again the fact of not touching you
a musty shroud around my shoulders.
Somewhere beyond the shadows you are
lurking deep in my emptiness.

My mind keeps striking matches in my soul
just to keep its undernourished bones warm.
Each step forward is a step further away
from where we once stood under the sun.
My father, and hopes for you, died that autumn.

Many forgetful seasons have since passed.
The shroud draped around my shoulders
have turned into rags. I'm still here.
Knowing you must be alive but nowhere
to be found is worse than death.

DUPONT CIRCLE, 3 A.M.

You sipped one watery drink after
another to the tune of stark laughter
echoing under the bar's rafters.

Some of the men stared your way,
and you fretted. But that was yesterday,
for you'd learned to dance alone anyway.

The bar closed with the pickings slim.
You are so relieved you're not like them.
The desperate grab your crotch on a whim.

The air, suddenly freed of cigarette smoke,
rushes into your lungs as if to choke,
but you scoff in your drying sweat soak.

A few blocks more of P Street, NW:
there at the end is an empty bench to rest
where late at night, alone with no one, is best.

Cars and Metrobuses revolve around you. Then
you close your eyes against the chill's yen.
You yawn, and you are no longer young again.

ON BLEECKER STREET

On Bleecker Street ghosts still roam lost, flitting:
beneath its white incisive paint and tar
aggrieved footsteps of Washington Irving,
Eugene O'Neill, and Henry James hide scars
of lives enraptured by the lure of pen.
Their ears absorbed loud cries of latest news,
fresh loaves, and eggs while they mused, *If not, then . . . ?*

On Bleecker Street horse dung smeared their old shoes,
reminding them what they had yet to write.
By kerosene or switch, they drew their blood's
unconscious pleasure, pulsing vividly
that present moment. Their tired eyes at night
shuttered, praying for dawn when words, in floods,
would flow, forgetting ghosts never break free.

IN THAT DARK OF NIGHT
for D.W., who said, "I want to feel your heartbeat in your lips."

1.

In that squinty dark of night I saw your eyes
gleam like charcoal ambers about to wisp
in a forest of overhanging dry smoke
emanating from the perfectly-appointed
owls whose eyes never flickered.
You looked every inch a weary traveler.

In you I suddenly found a map of ache
with destinations dotted by fireflies
bottled in your eyes. When you shook
my hand, the fireflies escaped everywhere
into a hovering campfire begging stories.
A log covered with cushy moss awaited.

Moonlight swayed across our searching faces
as we tried to hear each other above the din
of words from languages not quite our own.
How we came this far, what we've learned:
stories are the traveler's first aid kit
against loneliness of that road unmarked.

As wolves howled to the moon their mating calls,
our eyes twinkled steadily in their crossfire.

2.

In that distance of night your house stood
unlit. A mountain of chopped wood
cast a net of black across the driveway.
Above us you threw open a picnic blanket
of star crumbs that fell upwards to freeze
with the ache between us to kiss, to touch.

I felt along the dark wolfishness of your face,
the salt-and-pepper laughter in your goatee,
the sturdiness of your farmer's-tan chest,
the coarseness of your thumbs reaching
deep inside my shirt to rub my back fur.
The clear-eyed stars above blessed our first kiss.

Your unpainted house was an attic and garage
turned inside out as I followed you in:
every inch of shelf and table was covered
with remnants and fragments of junk,
dog-eared and tossed aside for that one
day you might suddenly find an use for.

I felt like a ghost resurrected
from a land never my own, nor named.

3.

Your bedroom was pitch-black. I could not see
your face. Holding you was a stranger to me,
never seeing but feeling the leathery skin
that held you all inside against mine, as your
arms surrounded me. I finally fell asleep
in the heaving forest of your slowing sighs.

In that neon of day, I awoke to find you
returning naked, a familiar stranger.
You crept like a baby into my arms,
resting your head on my bony shoulder.
I felt the sweat left over from the night,
another crumpled sheet beneath us.

I stared at your chiseled profile. A man
of stone and leather, you'd worked the land.
We walked through your yard and garden
holding hands while we talked of plants
you'd planted in even lines under the sun.
I am a tiny seed overlooked in an envelope.

That ache of day will find me planting
the right path to the one whose face reads home.

ODE TO U.S. 26

Bring back the stars once hanging so low
over the child's head that belonged to me.
Evergreens stood high like ragged crewcuts
in the face of angels spraying aurora borealis.
Each flutter of their wings caused another flush.
I blinked dreams. They flowered majestically
up there higher than any tree I had climbed.

Bring back the stunned deer's eyes staring astride
our unblinking lights before they leaped below
the bridge where the whiteness never ceased
murmuring. I prayed hard to become a doe,
bouncing my pogostick legs far into the woods.
I stared deep into the gray needles beyond
snowmobile trails punctuated by their hooves.

Bring back the steady black arrows pointing again
this way to Houghton, or that way back to Ironwood.
Each railroad crossing and pothole marked creaks
in the groans of my body's compass. I dreamed
the day I'd sit behind the chariot's wheel and race
against the thunderous pelts of rain and hail.
The radio's red light winked knowingly back at me.

Bring back the coldness seeping shivers
underneath my longjohns, terry socks, and mittens
as I sat tight for that slow fireplace warmth.

My tired eyes quavered in the flaming darts
of cars speeding to touch for a frightening second.
Their lights from around the bend unleashed forth
twin cauldrons of brilliance, clean and sharp.

LANCASTER COUNTY

1.

The horse wagon plods behind tourist cars
jangling with their 35mm cameras.
The Amish man tightens his jaw
as he shakes his reins a little more.

Their voices sift through the breeze;
they are awed by his grim silence.
He knows stories and secrets.
His eyes shrink from exposure.

2.

In a suburb nearby a Civic is filled with boxes,
packed with the all-in-the-name-of-Jesus touches.
The young woman rearranges in the trunk,
stretching like taffy empty centimeters to meters.

Her father's eyes watch from the porch windows;
she shoves some shoes into a side cave.
She knows stories and secrets.
Her eyes glare at his: never again.

3.

On the F train hurtling out of Manhattan,
she stands near two Hassidic Jews sitting.
Their wafer glasses are glued to their Talmuds
while FUCK YOU is sprawled in spray paint above them.

She hides her smile as the train slows.
The two men look up and give her a queer look.
She knows secrets and laughter:
home is suddenly a different concept.

REHOBOTH BEACH, 1985
for A.P.

How you'd massaged my burning back
          with vinegar:
                    your strong fingertips
   lent a shivery coolness
                      to my skin boiling still
    from the white sun
that hid so.

How we dove
          into the Atlantic's saltiness:
   the waves peppered us
                    into kids long neglected.
     The high roaring waves
                lifted me easily,
tossing me back to the shore,
            my legs now veined
            with dead kelp.

How I complained about
               my lightness: you laughed,
   your eyes shining
          brightly
as you reminded me of your solidness.

How I loved you: the waves dared again,
                  but I was never
     hurt. Not even
         once.

STILL LIFE WITH APPLE, PEARS, LEMONS, AND GRAPES, 1887
after Vincent Van Gogh at the Art Institute of Chicago

The place where his picture hung is empty,
a shadow of what could've been, a tasting
of fruit, love, scrumptiousness, a kiss.
Naked on that table, frameless, the canvas
exposed to the microscopic eyes of those
seeking flaws, cracks of age, rotting chemicals
is no longer stretched to embrace anyone.
The hours of ecstasy and sweat is a wreck
in a mirage of yawping years ready to rip, then tear.
Skins of such aching fruit ripen like cleavage.

You and I have become a still life painting,
full of shadows and sheen, paint chips peeling
until the original white lie is unblanketed,
unprotected with sun block against the toxin
of ultraviolet rays turning to sand and storm
threatening to tie-dye and die after being viewed
a thousand times and accidentally flashed
by yet another incompetent viewer's camera.
Minutes between us are centuries on the wall.
Someone, please deface me. I'm a forgery.

INEVITABILITY, 2005
in memory of our basset hound Elsa 1994 - 2007

One morning I will depart and leave her
behind with the man I once loved.
On the perch of her sofa near the door,
she will wait days and weeks as before,
sighing with her sleepy eyes fixed
on that door sure to click open suddenly
with my voice calling her once again.

How does anyone explain to a dog
the awful distance one must travel
not for just a few months but years
when all she knows are feet, treats,
and urine markings left behind by dogs
she's sniffed once or twice before?
Around the block is her domain.

One night I will return and meet her
wagging furiously in spite of her years,
her thick tender bones not as limber
with her fat pads that once slapped at
my hands when she lolled on her back.
Though her thinned face will have whitened,
she will insist on sniffing me, disbelieving.

I gaze into her chocolate-melted eyes,
warmed by the amber fire of familiarity.
Does she understand how I yearn for her
to be free of confusion when I finally go?
Will I ever be strong enough to look her
in the eye and lie that I've never left her?
I can't, can't put my heart to sleep like this.

PASSPORT

My name fills neatly inside the tiny boxes
I could never contain in my baggaged life.

My address feels fleeting. I belong to the sky,
where the clouds swell moodily as desire.

I list my parents' names, their birthdates.
It makes no other concession for their lives.

They check my photo ID against my face.
I am not a doctored illusion. I *exist*.

They staple my pristine birth certificate
to the form. I feel violated, my rights gone.

I am Kafka's Joseph K. in search of a trial,
something to give me a ticket of meaning.

After years of dreaming, I find my life ending
on a blank line. I am more than a signature.

PALLETS

In the dingy warehouse shell-shocked
by bitter words of divorce and death,
the cement floor is worn smooth,
crisscrossed from black rubber tires.
The floor is a topographic map.
In one corner of yet another country
soon to be conquered, a valley
of sentimentalities, a nation's pride,
a cemetery plot marked, is a tall box.

Years have taught these men how to pack
so nothing would break, not like
their souls broken like eggshells,
seeping into composts near gardens
never theirs to grow in the first place.
All they've got left is the waft of dreams
so hallucinatory it keeps them awake
for days when their wives close
thighs in the hour of constant need.

In their hands are hammers and mouthfuls
of nails ready to seal each upright coffin
only to be dismantled in another warehouse
in a country different from this.
The spoils of war are easily rotted.
Go, my dear pallet, go with God.

NEW YORK 1988 - 2005

I strip the gritty city clean of my kisses.
It will be mine to keep as I weep dreams.
Leaving is much easier than I ever expected.

From this point on, I will drape my shroud
about my soul and walk forth in the dark.
No one warned me of such ease of glide.

As constant as fireflies hint at a flame
so fleetingly mine and gone too soon,
I will give my life a map, a name.

I strap on my sandals and survey the sunset.
My heart bobs like a lost loon on the lake
while bats slash skidmarks across the sky.

My hands are rich with the ache of touch.
I am bereft of a love to call my own.
The moon does not light my hapless way.

I have nothing to show for my years gone
except a weariness that's dampened my feet.
I leave behind a trail sure to evaporate.

PENITENT

Simply that you wouldn't take what I'd felt:
   a fossil spun,
lines embedded in my palms,
     a struck match gone,
winters of gray aching for spiteful green,
   a crooked chair,
nights spent online with strangers,
     a smudged baseball,
words ephemeral as perfume sprayed young,
   a drab river
stilled while birthing mosquitoes,
     a rub of sweat
poised to glide across taut power cables
   from brow to tongue,
endless blinks of white ribbon
     a dotted line
down the road that shakes clean to names unsaid,
   the champagne fizz
relentless and hesitant
     to brush the air
chokeful as exhaust pipes spewing octaves,
   sharp somersaults
in perfect trampoline's pulse,
     a brittle twig
wedded to pneumonia's bed of leaves,
   a clap unheard,

the red in emergency
     signs to pump blood
in veins all rivulets of drought unskeined,
    a book's exposed
thighs under the looking glass,
    a gap between
railroad tracks laid to lasso the last car,
    hands together
an inch apart from clinging
     for salvation.

JULES

St. Mark's Place may yawn and turn over
for another day of new trends and eateries.
In our minds Jules is an old-friend place.

Supposing the stars never change,
we'll always hear Nino Rota breathe once
again with Yuri the accordionist

donning his kooky wigs and glasses.
French movie posters will litter our eyes
as we huddle in this bistro of bonhomie.

The atmosphere and attitude is all
that's left as we avoid talking
about our past. It is now a museum.

THE ACHE OF ALCHEMY

1.

Time is mercury. It slithers from one beaker
to another in the glare of constant monitoring.
Its alchemy flashes our glass masks as we record
our detailed observations. It rises and drops
when we recall how brilliant its silverness looked
in the early days of our lives. We were fooled
into thinking it would forever gleam. We played
games of growing up tall enough to be in the lab.
Textbooks from our parents comprised our studies.
The toughest was always chemistry of the heart.
We were always amazed when we were handed
keys to the Great Lab, only to be disappointed
by how clumsy all our experiments had been.
Mercury has become radioactive. We wear masks,
not daring to breathe its elusiveness. We pour
again and see it evaporate. We are obsolescent.

2.

Memory is an old machine. Nothing ever works.
It coughs up the weirdest smells that recall
taste of momentous discoveries. It sparks
tears in our eyes when it lights up images
cobwebbed in the attic of our lives. It hums
lost happy tunes when we stop to listen.
It jumps suddenly when we feel our pulses
slow down to uselessness. We jolt awake.
We unscrew the shell off grime-ridden parts.
Nothing seems to fit, yet it grinds gracefully.
We sit for hours watching, already forgetting.
It bangs us with force when we feel our bodies
slow down and sag. We kick it non-stop.
It is a cruel machine with no conscience.
But we cannot bear to toss it out. We've learned
to ache for the mysterious industry of its soul.

IN EDINBURGH CASTLE

Tourists with clicky digital
cameras hanging swaggle
up the lugubrious Lawnmarket
past the castle's staunch shoulders.
We are ants in search of morsels.
But I do not flock to frenzy
in fingerpointed exclamations.

They are too busy popping
well-lit exhibits and rooms
led by curvy steps worn
down by centuries of death,
intrigue, and power.
My heart's a hidden exhibit,
lined with the cork of rage.

No tapestry of us will hang
in the echoey dining hall.
The wool and dye are infested
with maggots misunderstanding.
Stoneworn faces staring
do not flinch when they trickle
down tears of insects buzzing.

The shadows of your touch
clang deep. A thousand bells
toll our death, and no one
lists our salient facts. We are
history. Never mind. Time
to move on to the next
exhibit. The camera flashes.

ST. PAUL'S CATHEDRAL, LONDON

Hold me from afar, I say. The river beyond
us is hurt and angry. The miles of snake
is a Thames disconnected,
its chopped bits writhing about for blood.
The sky quakes, quivers.
Clouds fall. We are covered
in gauzes of gray and white.

Water hurls its shrapnel at our eyes.
In the blitzed blur we stumble,
our feet kludgy maps home
past each other until the cathedral
lifts her veil to find you standing
there with your bandaged eyes gazing
past me should the river reconnect.

PIRATES

Trace the lines of cartography
across the seven seas of my palms.

Nerve endings beneath the skin are
ports where my desires anchor.

Tattoo my body with your tongue.
Make it swear worse than sailors.

Stow away the loot of your eyes.
It hurts to steal a glance from you.

Cool me with promises of the plank.
Sharks lurk among dolphins.

I'm patched with sweaty islands.
Volcanoes can erupt at any second.

Unroll the map of routes between us.
Timing's everything, you say.

Take off your silly eye patch.
We're no longer ink and skin.

PIGEONS
for Suzanne Easton Steele-Mueller 1921 - 2008

Through the snowflake-kissed air the pigeons soar
when slim peckings appear along the old quay,
now concrete ghosts of wooden docks decayed.

Constant feedings from the summer before
have accumulated in fat gray breasts,
now pillowy shelves for their sleepy heads.

They cluster hours on branches, brittle beds
shaken by fierce weather and the homeless
figuring them tasty enough for game.

They shiver ice inside their skins and wings,
puffing until a sailor's woman sings
of pining winters for her long-dead flame.

Her desperate mourning never buries.
But how they've broken sleep: hungry flurries.

ON A GREENPOINT PIER
after F.T.

Look how the East River flows,
wrapping waves
around faltering piers.
They haven't collapsed,
yet.
I watch the sun bounce
off the greenness,
that cold blueness
a fickle mirror of Manhattan
at night.
Huge tugboats drift.
I search them for signs
of life, a man.
There is none.
Beyond the ships the skyline
is gray, covered with
the smoke
from its thousand factories
of dreamers.
The river ploughs
ripple after ripple
below me
as I glance back
on India Street.
The apartment buildings
have hung white clothes

al fresco.
They are waving.
The river is fleeing
the ocean,
that size of mysterious
everything.
I too have fled
this street
a long time ago.
But I have still no home
to which to flee.
The river starts here.

BEFORE STATEN ISLAND, 1989

The ferry is waiting for me to drop in
a quarter, for a plodding ride in the winds
washing past the Statue of Liberty.
As I stand behind the railing, a memory

returns the sureness of your pure chin:
touching it once, I have never been the same since
you left. So what if I've slept with others in
the meantime? The turnstiles are waiting for money,

the ferry is waiting,
and I'm still waiting for you to drop in
at my place, blubbering, "Sorry, thought I had you pinned
down," and take me into your arms. Nothing comes free,

or had you always thought I could be had for free?
The harbor opens up to swallow your memory—
or tries to—as I turn to face the sharp winds
on the ferry. I'm waiting.

IN BATTERY PARK CITY

I will forget you. The Hudson River says so:
lights of New Jersey and condos cast a cool glow
on the waters. It is not your face
I see on its surfaces but the empty embrace
of you when I told you, angrily, to go.

The river reminds me: it knows also
that those new buildings could let go
of its steel beams. Anytime. Anyplace.

I will forget you,
not wondering whether your looks have remained so
when I turn your age. By then I will know
whether I can recall your nakedly hesitant face,
whether a more giving man has claimed your place,
whether I continue to seek your praise.

The winds give the river its flickering glow.
I will forget you.

AFTER SUDDENLY SEEING A.R. AGAIN

And you—what have you become in the years
    gone by? You have become a mask,
scraggly with a scotch-colored beard of losses.
    I have this black-and-white image
of you laughing and hanging on to your hat
    while beyond the Vesuvius volcano.
You are a Pompeiian spirit frozen in time.

    I think of you now sitting at home,
your wrapped joint perched in the clawhole
    of some Art Deco glass ashtray,
as you flick the remote for carefully-assembled
    scenes waiting to shatter your
imagination. I was perhaps too young, uninformed
    then. Those years had such a mileage.

I wandered lost among the dust-choked alleys
    of the Gaza Strip. I survived a war
of illegal passports, martial blockades,
    and confiscated weapons.
Whatever happened to the ease of entry?
    Your eyes once held gate signs
that said I didn't need identification.

Yet officials interrogated me
until they could map the points of my psyche
   where they could next dismantle.
They have flung open every safe deposit drawer
   in my memory vaults: you are
only a spectral moonbeam, a vacant mask haunting
   no longer my ashy twilights.

SWEET HIGHWAY
for Robert Giard 1940 - 2002

You never learned to drive. Never knew why,
but there you stood, camera in hand,
steady as a wizened truck driver
behind the steering wheel. Your eye
hungered for whatever light fell on my face,
years ago when I didn't know my future.
I was a tourist lost in a bad neighborhood.
As I stood there, wondering where I was
to go with my unmapped smile, you lit up.
Your face was a well-worn Baedeker's guide,
and I felt right at home in front of you,
even when the draft of winter snaked in from
the window where I stood. I wonder,
as I did then, how you could mark the terrain
of my indecisiveness, my elusive soul,
all over the contact sheets you sent me.
I thought of your darkroom and its many secrets
aswirl and arising to the blood-silver surface,
and how much light it took to expose faces.
Your billboard images will forever thunder by
like Mack delivery trucks already late,
even when you became a heart attack
on that bus from Minneapolis to Chicago,
an unexpected click of the other camera,
left gaping in the darkroom of my soul.

APARTMENT HUNTING

Each step unfamiliar across
the floor is a constant introduction.

Each wall tries to erase ghosts
of cheap pictures once hung.

Each closet rod sags and cowers
in the glare of swinging hangers.

Each light bulb hiccups open,
its eyelid in a dreary droop.

Each doorknob twists open
secrets long ziplocked shut.

Each window breathes in
a hopeful breeze that sways.

Each place is an orphanage.
Its children are poised, waiting.

SHELTER

1.

Off Black River Harbor I wade the shore,
cuffs of my pants rolled up on my shins.
The water is no longer murky as decades ago.
My toenails are the same color as pale agates
swirling past my feet. I scan each ebb
of waves for the most eye-catching stones
left behind in the exodus towards north.
I pull out the front hem of my T-shirt and hold it up
as I cradle one abandoned stone after another.
Lake Superior is an orphanage.

2.

My bathroom counter is lined with these stones.
I keep them there to remind me of summer days
when I treaded for rocks streaked with mercury blood,
mottles of tan and cream, and glints of diamond tears.
How they'd once shimmered in the waves
even as they'd begged for mercy. I douse them
in tap water, but fluorescent counter lights strip dry
away the last of their lives. They do not shine.
I am homeless.

SMITH CREEK
for K.A.

It keeps calling to me.
It knows my one name no one else knows.
The waves keep surging no matter
how small and shallow they are.
Not even ice can break their spirit.
Each wave does not have a name,
but together they know mine. They know
the seasons of my dreams. I am
a chunk of ice spinning helplessly
into the vertigo of nowhere.
Trees and plants pay me no heed.
Each day they worship the little waves
constantly waving good-bye
in this parade of farewells.
How little these waves know,
and how nameless I forever remain.
I will soon melt into a wave
like so many others.

MOSS IN MUIR WOODS

It is a demanding cloak,
arms of a child hugging

the waists of tired trees.
Their foreheads sop wet

in the redwood sweatshops
overlooking the Pacific.

I stroke it. The moss yields
tenderly under my fingers.

I remember what it means
to leave home, and to return.

THE NOMADS
for R.C.

It started way back when we were young, wanting
new games to play under the flaps of our tent;
we called each other's name at least a
dozen times before finding sleep each night.

Our sandals always split in the dry sun and
slippery dunes on the Sahara's edge. There we
sat, flattening fat flies with crusty
thumbs, and told each other where we'd each go.

You wanted America. It sounded so
exciting, what with commercial jingles in
English for Coca-Cola on Father's
transistor radio with its static.

You mimicked words, not knowing what they all meant.
What mattered was the *tone*, those strange accents of
Hollywood gossip and Dick Clark's suave
questions on record ratings from Philly.

So: one day in Cairo forty years ago
you simply vanished; I knew to where you'd gone.
I had no reason to cry but both
Father and Mother wept moonlit nights: *why?*

Our camels gazed back at us with bored eyes. I
knew it would be a long, long time before you'd come
back with stories of magical lands.
Time found me two wives who gave me ten children.

We lived among the changing geography,
fierce winds peltering the dunes into worthless
landmarks. At night we saw the sureness of
stars, and they guided us to more barters.

Wherever we went, Father and Mother looked
for you; even the sun couldn't dry their tears
quickly enough in those lone moments.
But I pulled them on. *We've got to move on.*

Your silence broke Mother's heart. Finally we
stopped moving, and spent three luminous weeks of
her voice and hands clinging to Father's.
When she died, I knew she'd fly where you were.

Two years on, Father stood before me and said,
It's time. I took command of our tribe, swollen
to thirteen mouths to feed along with
nine camels. Their warm milk kept us alive.

Before the Nile rose again, I went to the
place where I saw you last, the back of your head
nodding with a pale American
and his wife; I wondered how you'd met them.

Young chickens squalled among tethered goats as I
sought you. The crowd's din caused me to long for
steadfast hums of fine sand grains beating
against my robes, my dear camel; then I stopped.

You had been left for dead: your scruffy crewcut,
crow's feet, and thick moustache made you look different.
Could you be the same one? I blinked, and
I *knew*. You were sleeping off a stupor.

Your jeans were torn in the knees; you had been robbed
of passport and money. Flies settled on the drool
from your mouth. I called out your name, the
familiar echoes from misplaced dunes.

Your eyes woke, sadly, at me as I pulled you
up into our sudden embrace. How I'd missed
holding you like this, my dear brother!
You sputtered out in English, *Oh screw it!*

I covered you with my swaths and forced your arms
around me as I kicked my camel towards
my wives and sons. But they looked at you
strangely; they couldn't see my face in you.

You gave up jeans for robes anyway and joined
us for another season of sand and stars.
New York and L.A. were your new tales
late at night while the fire soothed our worn souls.

There must be an oasis for tired men like us.
Our minds concoct mirages out of nothing
but scraps of hearsay and bad static.
That's why we cannot rest until we find it.

ALL WE'VE GOT LEFT
for A.P., a deafblind man

Your feet tread across the sliced red bricks
on the way home in the dark. How hard
it must've been at first to learn each step,
tentative at first and then memorizing
each potential danger in daylight,
your body remembering under the streetlamps.

Years ago when we were both young,
we somehow found our way to each other.
Your hand stayed gently under my elbow.
The blue-gray clouds drifting above us
never once rained down on the sidewalks.
I never told you that they hung there.

Your city remains a monument to sadness
with no plaque to summarize for tourists
happening to waltz in with their guidebooks.
Memories are kangaroos springing through
the night. You see all but you catch none
long enough to sleep in its pouch.

My years with you back then were small
as the rowhouses huddled together.
The balmy winds chased after the stars
I couldn't see past the brilliant streetlamps.

How I slept dawns only to find damp
kisses clinging to the side of my neck.

Each time I visit your city, my youth fades
slowly as I walk along the streets of Dupont Circle,
leaving behind empty shells of dreams I held
once to my poor anxious heart. These days
I wear a raincoat and carry an old umbrella.
All we've got left are the years that will never dry.

STRANGERS FAMILIAR ON EAST 11TH STREET

Each month brings me more and more
ghosts once known
in the flesh when I lived there
on that street.
They'll never know my name
as we pass
unexpectedly after
years. Did we know each other's
faces while
waiting in line for our stamps,
or bumping
each other in East Village,
perhaps on
St. Mark's Place when it belonged
to the scuzz
with mohawks, dyed hair, earrings,
mascara,
and clots of acne on pale skin?
Or did we
cruise each other with a smile,
only that
we'd never shook hands and talked?
We are ghosts
rushing to somewhere else than
forgetting.

KEEPSAKE

Once in a while you forget
it's there on the shelf.
A memento from some summer.

After all you have so many things
littering everywhere you look.
Seasons leave behind crumpled paper.

This is what happens when years
roll by. Such waters move still.
Your memory hasn't frozen quite yet.

There it is. Blow the dust off.
It's yours. Has always been.
Summer's a wind waiting to kiss again.

SOME DAYS

Your name is whispered, a ghost on my lips.
Years have passed since I saw you last.

Racing by highway flares, I see your face.
Then I catch my blindness in the dashboard mirror.

Gusts of wind run off with my last road map,
a handkerchief kiting up into the clouds.

Gone are the roads when dreams of you
spread like wildfire all over my body.

I no longer consider myself a tourist.
My heart's not the camera it used to be.

The stars in my eyes have turned into sand.
The atlas of you is gone. I'm grateful.

Having lost direction, I become a landmark.
Your silence voices legends they imagine.

ROAD WORK AHEAD

Supposing the road had never been mine
I would've traveled anyway with you
past points of tenderness between our minds.
The map wouldn't have been different or new;
I'd still discover peaks, waysides, picture-
taking of sights to last forever in
my scrapbook: look at how many pictures
have framed my broken life. Needles and pins
propel me to drive down the lonely road
for you, or past you; who are you to me?
All those years of misintentions have shown
the art of promising a fallacy:
why, the road bleeds. Look how it calls me back,
back to my heart whose home I've always lacked.

TO MY WEARY TRAVELER

Soothe your eyes upon my lit windows
late at night; you've traveled
enough all those years on the road.
The silence of speedometers is hell.
Come on in, my dear traveler;
unravel in my fat chair like a river
whose dam is breaking. Your face
is a map, an emotional suitcase;
hot chocolate should loosen you more.
Please. Do not act surprised or amazed.
It is you I have been waiting for.

My house's taken on such a happy glow
since you arrived. More? Swell.
Here you go. More marshmallows?
Unravel the tales you've wanted to tell
but never could. So you have no lover?
Please. Do tell me where you were,
or his memory you cannot erase . . .
So he laughed when you'd offered a case
of champagne and that something more?
No. No matter how you've lost face,
it is you I have been waiting for.

The kerosene lamp flickers and flows
with each booming laugh of your belly.
I want to hear all the jokes you know.

And listen: that's the church bell
tolling twelve times across the river.
That's a reminder for fated lovers
to caress each other's bodies and faces
one more time before they deflate
into a pair of hands married for more.
I stroke lightly your wrinkled face.
It is you I have been waiting for.

I once loved someone years ago,
but he left me standing here. Well.
He was always the one for the road.
Here's your room, and your towels.
Do not try dreaming of your ex-lover;
sleep sweetly this night like no other
as you wipe his kisses from your face.
Allow my pillows to rest their case.
I turn out lamps, one after another,
while I meditate on your peaceful face.
It is you I have been waiting for.

Please do stay here for another day.
Allow me to draw a new map, a new slate,
while my tea kettle sits ready to pour.
And do bring in all your suitcases.
It is you I have been waiting for.

ABOUT THE AUTHOR

Raymond Luczak was raised in Ironwood and Houghton, Michigan. At seven months, he lost much of his hearing due to double pneumonia and a high fever.

He holds a B.A. in English from Gallaudet University in Washington, D.C. In 1990 his essay "Notes of a Deaf Gay Writer" appeared as a cover story in *Christopher Street*; it was recently expanded as *Notes of a Deaf Gay Writer: 20 Years Later* (Handtype Press). Alyson Books commissioned him to edit *Eyes of Desire: A Deaf Gay & Lesbian Reader*, which received two nominations for the Lambda Literary Award. Fourteen years later he edited its sequel *Eyes of Desire 2: A Deaf GLBT Reader* (Handtype Press).

His poetry collections include *St. Michael's Fall* (Deaf Life Press), *This Way to the Acorns* (The Tactile Mind Press), and *Mute* (A Midsummer Night's Press). His poetry has earned him an Artist Recognition Grant from the Jerome Foundation and VSA Minnesota. His novel *Men with Their Hands* (Queer Mojo) won a first-place grant from the Arch and Bruce Brown Foundation for Full-Length Fiction 2003 and first place in the Project: QueerLit 2006 Contest.

Nineteen of Luczak's stage plays have been performed in America, Canada, and England. Four of them are collected in *Whispers of a Savage Sort and Other Plays about the Deaf American Experience* (Gallaudet University Press). As a filmmaker, he has directed two full-length documentaries (*Guy Wonder: Stories & Artwork and Nathie: No Hand-Me-Downs*) and worked with the renowned storyteller Manny Hernandez (*Manny ASL: Stories in American Sign Language*).

He lives in Minneapolis, Minnesota.

www.raymondluczak.com

ABOUT THE PUBLISHER

The mission of Sibling Rivalry Press is to develop, publish, and promote outlaw artistic talent—those projects which inspire people to read, challenge, and ponder the complexities of life in dark rooms, under blankets by cell-phone illumination, in the backseats of cars, and on spring-day park benches next to people reading Plath, Ginsberg, and Whitman. We welcome manuscripts which push boundaries, sing sweetly, or inspire us to perform karaoke in drag. Not much makes us flinch.

For more information, visit us online.

www.siblingrivalrypress.com